The Painted Lady

Also by Suzanne Edgar

Canberra Tales (with Seven Writers), reissued as *The Division of Love*

Counting Backwards

The Love Procession

The Painted Lady

Suzanne Edgar

Indigo

Acknowledgements

Many of these poems have been published, in:
the *Adelaide Review, ACTWrite, Artlook,* the *Australian's Review of Books, Eureka Street, Muse, Quadrant, The Weekend Australian.*

They have appeared in these anthologies:
National Library of Australia, *Canberra Arts Anthology,* 1999;
J.M. Bean et al. eds, *Bird Before Landing,* 2002;
End of Season, Lulu Books, USA, 2003; Vee Malnar ed., *First Breath,* 2004; Margaret Bradstock ed., *Suburbs of the Mind,* 2004;
Les Murray ed., *Best Australian Poems 2004* and *Best Australian Poems 2005*;
Rob Walker and Louise Nicholas eds, *Friendly Street Poets Thirty,* 2006.

They have been read at:
Friendly Street Poets, Adelaide; Poetry at the Red Belly Black Café, Canberra; the Art Gallery of South Australia; Nolan Gallery; and the National Gallery of Australia, Canberra.

'Uriarra' and 'Night Shift' won the C.J. Dennis literary award for poetry in 2002 and 2003.

I am indebted to my colleague-friends who meet at The Mull and Fiddle: Martin Dolan, Melinda Smith and Michael Thorley; without them this book would not exist. I have also received valued support from Darryl Bennet and Di Langmore at the *Australian Dictionary of Biography*; from Louise Nicholas, and from Dorothy Horsfield and Dorothy Johnston of the old Seven Writers group.
To my husband Peter, heartfelt thanks.

The writing of this book was assisted by a grant from artsACT.

The Painted Lady
ISBN 978 1 74027 398 5
Copyright © text Suzanne Edgar 2006
Copyright © cover design Anne Langridge 2002

An Indigo book first published 2006
Reprinted with revisions 2007
Reprinted 2016

GINNINDERRA PRESS
PO Box 3461 Port Adelaide 5015
www.ginninderrapress.com.au

for Zara

Contents

Love Poem	11
Breasts	12
Nightfall	13
Valentine	14
Tale of a Fox	15
I'm Keeping These	16
The Quarrel	17
Home Alone	18
Mirror Image	19
Still Life with Portrait	20
Above the Shop	22
Sea Acres	23
Sting	24
A Piece of Advice	26
The Flirting	28
Birth Control	30
The Loneliness of Salt	31
Sweet Peas	32
Wind-flowers	33
Stalker	34
Legacies I	35
Legacies II	37
The Dwindling	39
The Bone Tree	41
Private Museum	43
Night Shift	46
The Dance	48
The Birds	49
Spoonbills, Wooli	50
Timbarra	51

The Weaver	52
Uriarra	53
Platypus	54
Meeeting the Psyllid	55
Wistaria	56
Fossils, Wee Jasper	57
Heat	58
This Rain	60
Eviction	61
Prodigal Son	63
The Trial	64
For my Son	65
The Scholar and the Wren	66
Red Madonna	67
Soup Kitchen	69
Cuisine Minceur	70
Leaves	71
The True Café	73
The Queue	75
The Skater	76
Chica	77
The Burqa	79
Kongarati Cave	80
Wangangu	81
The Patriarch's House by the Sea	82
Old Dubbo Gaol, 2004	83
Lament for London Bus No. 30, 2005	84
Voyeur	85
Erhu Player, Sydney	86
The Ring Maker	87
The Bookbinder	88
The Tide	90
The Model and her Model	91

Enid on the Sofa, 1957	92
Painted Lady	93
The Collector	95
Beguiled	96
Harpy	97
Flesh and Bone	98
Two Good Men	100
Flight	102
Seasons	103
Under the Jacaranda Tree	104
New Baby	105
Inheritance	106
Grandmother	107
What Women Want	108
Rushcutters Walk	109
Under the Magnolia Tree	110
After Vermeer	111

Love Poem

I love a stickiness that follows
the perfume of petunias,
a Red Gum encrusted
with its own shed skin,
the wraith of a cobweb tethered
by one light foot to the roof
and the hooting of coots
along the lake at dusk.

That fine fur
on the skin of a peach
is your arm against mine
in our clean-sheeted bed.
Street lamps flicker on,
I strain to hear
the hum of your car
returning at night
with the kiss to come.

When I am old and slow
I shall rake the sound
of gravel in your voice
singing at the piano,
unpack these gifts
and play with them
like a lonely child
shuffling her cards
on the rumpled quilt.

Breasts

Late at night my breasts
push on the dividing wall,
whisper through cracks in the lace.
When I let them out of their cage
they moan with pleasure, swing free
and tumble down the steps of my ribs
to laugh and sigh
at the soft, reviving kiss of air.
While I sleep these milk-white
tipsy creatures sidle and sway,
eavesdrop, round-eyed,
on dreams and night games.
At first light they wait, subdued
for the blindfold, the cage, separation
and a stretch of solitary confinement.

Nightfall

The street lamp is lost in shimmer,
the path thick with almond flowers.
Shadows make way for my feet
on the worn stone steps.

There is even a moth to surprise me
turning its back, as a Bogong will,
in that quiet cranny
between wall and door.

I walk in – to music, light, this man
gutting fish for food,
a river-damp bag at his feet.
Wine cools in the well of the sink.

Where else would I go,
with night fallen soft as moth's wing?
We fold ourselves together
like two hands in prayer.

Valentine

You ask me if there'll ever be a time
when I begin to fret and tire of you,
when wanderlust might drive me to pursue
a daily pattern with a different rhyme.
Some women would not think it such a crime
to take a secret lover (even two).
These women hanker after something new
and snatch it, if they can, when in their prime.
But I intend to love you to the end,
enjoy adventures in a different way.
Seeking my pleasure with a thousand men
through paintings, books and films, I'll learn to spend
my fund of love so no one has to pay
and rule myself by this fair regimen.

Tale of a Fox

i.m. Ted Hughes

I love to hear this man's hypnotic tone
escape the grooves of a vinyl forty-five.
Filling my room it warms me to the bone,
a disembodied voice that comes alive
with accents slow, deliberate and deep
to punctuate each perfect lilting line.
It makes me long to have his thrusting lip
push apart the welcoming curve of mine.
I often play a favourite poem over,
dwell on every word and think it through:
know the fox he speaks of like a lover,
see it mount the rise, come into view
with neat black paws that print the white of snow –
the poet watching from a room below.

I'm Keeping These

I know my way around your foot,
its naked, supple-leather touch
is there to greet me in the morning bed.
I would not pass through dreaming night
without your foot beside me.
Late at night in a quiet room
I listen for your step.
That old, familiar, heavy tread
belongs to me.

Your whistle in the corridor
and hand with rocky knuckles
closing over mine, hair
in the furrow of your neck –
these, too, belong to me
and I am on my guard,
defending them from raids
by light-fingered women,
pickpockets or body-snatchers.
I've given freely in exchange,
anything that took your fancy:
adoring eyes, the suck of flesh,
hilarious laughter on the stair.

It's always been my habit
to enter all your virtues
in my account book.
Browsers may unearth the records
but I do not bequeath them
to any who come after.
They go with me.

The Quarrel

The weep of his shoulders caught me,
I'd never seen him sad before.
Also, the way he ignored the dog.

She fell back
to droop along,
head down and tongue lolling.

The baggy grey sweater
hung over his behind.
I like a man with a neat, tight bum.

His arms swung loose, too,
and he stumbled often
in a way I couldn't recall.

The dust of our quarrel filled the air
like an orange cloud of pride
blurring the space between us.

When he passed the red car
he dropped my last note
and trod it underfoot.

His hair lifted and fell
in the spiteful wind
that flew down our street.

At the corner he stopped
to look over his shoulder
but this time I did not wave.

He shrugged, turned
and disappeared.
The last thing was the tail of the dog.

Home Alone

When I am home alone
the rooms subside and settle with a sigh,
I hear the breathing of the fridge, that tap.
Our house is mine, for now,
and I'm a kindly ruler,

the only law is solitude.
I can forget to dress,
I write in bed and read while eating,
open all the doors
to let in light and air.

Time stretches generously.
I take another chocolate,
turn the Schubert up
at both ends of our house
and leave a book on every chair.

I stroke my walls in passing,
notice self-effacing pictures,
become so friendly with the place
I even wash its kitchen floor
and clean the window with the view.

Alone, I meet myself again,
discover misplaced thoughts
and talk with favourite birds.
These are the games I play when safe,
knowing you'll come home.

Mirror Image

When I dust and polish pictures
that line my house's walls
I return the light of day
to the women of the family
who wait there under glass.

My mirrored eyes go walking
in one aunt's embroidered garden,
round another's pastel sketch
of her model's languid pose;
meet a daughter's watercolour,
plums and candle flame;
come to rest upon my mother,
that uncertain sepia bride.

My work is never lasting
for lustre fades with time.
The humble art of cleaning
is never framed or hung
and following my hand,
the new motes drifting down
re-seal the household shrines.

Still Life with Portrait

I compose the still life, along a shelf:
a small glass vase like a trumpet,
white wind-flowers on green stems.
In the glow of the lamp
these flowers lift your eyes
to cream and green in the portrait above,
a portrait of my sister in Seville.
The dark hair has been brushed
back and fastened at the nape,
she could be Spanish, or Frida Kahlo.
Her burnt-almond stare is defiant
with love for the student who paints her
in the high-backed green chair,
a pale scarf foaming at her throat.
Neither my sister nor the artist
who was soon to leave her
knew she would die young.

Here, she's confined in a plain pine frame
behind my letter-rack with postcards:
a fruit-dove, a Botticelli Venus.
In the soft light their rosy colours,
the feathered breast of the bird,
the angel-woman's cheek and lips,
shine like my brass candlestick –
stars twinkle in the porcelain.

Flowers, lamp and candlestick
rest upon a tracery of lace
overlapping the rim of the shelf
like an altar cloth in a holy place,
a place where voices rise and fall
where light is strained through coloured glass
and people sing of everlasting life.

Above the Shop

If I went back to that dead-end lane
I'd find the smears of chicken grease,
meet tomcats sharp and skinny as rats
and smell the bloody rabbit fur.
A service lane in a seaside town
and backside to the high street shops,
it was never walked by any man
who had no business there.

I'd open the gate to a yard with sheds
tacked on behind my father's shop,
see Herbie plucking headless chooks
and Theo peeling spuds for chips.
Boards that creak in the wooden stairs
might stop me in my tracks
before I reach my father's den
where cashbooks with their copperplate
show profit, loss and poor return.
Red cushions line a cane settee
for the girl who washes floors downstairs
and comes for him on sultry nights.

On his desk the Rotary wheel
spelt out its four-way ethical test,
a feel-good guide for truth and justice
meant to benefit all concerned.
My mother, often known to my dad
as Lady Muck of the Fowl Yard,
was not, of course, a Rotarian –
the roughest seas beyond the pier
never reached that oil-slick lane
to rinse away the grease.

Sea Acres

On a soldier-settler's paltry coastal block
the Halls ran scraggy sheep on limestone soil
though wool was cheap and set to stay that way.
They built a few cement and iron shacks
and called it a Happy Holiday Farm for kids.
Riding an old black mare called Little Jet,
I learned to weave through scrub and round up stock.
My father caught fish, my mother read her books
and taught herself to use a mean wood stove.
Each May we drove the pebbled peninsular road
joking and singing, scared of bursting a tyre,
until things blew apart, back home in town.
My father said he couldn't take much more
and acted on his scarlet woman's plan
to head up north and buy a run-down pub.
No one spoke of holiday trips to the bush
when I moved out to share a flat with friends.
Adrift in all that spooky solitude,
my mother wanted to try a fresh start –
but Dad refused to give it another go.
Unlike the farm, there wasn't much left of use,
nothing to salvage and build again from scrap.

Sting

You were my dark-haired mother
cutting spikes of lavender
for empty summer bedrooms
when a bee spun out to sting you
and then, next year, another…
there was a pattern to it.
Every year a sulky bee
would punish your soft flesh,
sink its venom and stage
its final exit at your feet.
Choked by a blue, fat tongue,
you struggled for breath,
for life in the scented garden.

The next could be your last, they said,
arranging your injections
for the closing in of winter.
A dry, hard winter,
too harsh for gardens; too cold
to chafe a spirit craving sun
and the voices of children.
Still you trudged, gut-lonely,
for those needles against
a sting with your name on it
until the night you decided –

to cheat the needle and the bee
and choose an easier poison,
one you delivered yourself.
After which, like any honey-winged
and woundful thing
you fell into a fatal sleep,
behind closed blinds,
in your house set back
among lavender bushes.

A Piece of Advice

There's a problem for the suicide,
she never stays awake to hear
how the plot works out.
Never hears who's in the will
or if the scarlet woman earns
the bitterness of just deserts.
Doesn't see her daughter
bear another daughter
to match her missing forebear's look:
the curious, dark and darting eyes,
her olive skin and tiny frame.

A suicide can't enjoy
the taste she meant to relish:
you'll be sorry,
now look what you made me do,
taunts that might have been
a good result for one like her
whose choices narrowed down
to twenty capsules spilt across
the ridges of a draining board.
Neither will she know about
a husband's troubled end,
the lasting smart of guilt
working its sure way in.

Despair defeats the suicide –
the body isn't found in time,
it cannot be revived.
This woman won't be there
to tell the gist of it,
the unromantic truth
about the waste of such a step
and all that she has lately learned:
it's wise to only try to die.

The Flirting

It was the best adventure,
my journey through the garden
that stepped in level terraces
down, from ridge to gully,
to Grandpa's dangerous dunny
with gaping, unlatchable door.
Redback spiders lay in wait
to watch me perching, tilted
over the risky edge of its hole.
And then, just outside
among the crimson waratahs,
a deeper hole was waiting
under cover of a lid.
He shot a snake, once,
swimming round and around
that black well.

So he boarded it up
to stop the kids from drowning
with the red-bellied black.
But there were slits that winked
from splintered timber.
If you squatted down
and peered in to darkness,
the dread was thrilling.
Enough to make you scramble
up the gravelled slope
to kitchen, wood stove,
the calmly waiting face
of Grandma stirring porridge.
Living out on the plains,
I mourn them all:
dunny, well, wood stove,
and the fast electric charge
from forbidden flirting.

Birth Control

I want no more
children, Walter,
my grandmother said
after her third was born.
And he never
touched me again
my dear,
from that day to this.

Thirty years without touching.
Not even looking.
Feather bed and flannelette,
living by the rules
of the Rotary wheel.
Mysterious times of silence
in the small, dank bathroom
behind a locked door.

His daughters were seen
but not heard by Walter McVey
who dried on the vine
like the muscatel grapes
he grew but never ate.
And Grandma laughed,
My dear, she said,
I never gave it a thought.

The Loneliness of Salt

Wanting the comfort of waves,
my aunt looks out to sea.
From inside her cocoon car
she stares and stares,
waiting for salt solace.

She has left her cold house,
her days of filing the office,
nights with just the wireless.
No more Father, not even Mother.
Home is dry as old bread in her mouth.

I could say she's a bone-thin beast
dragging slow feet to the salt-lick,
hind leg lame,
no brisk wife to grab a pinch of salt
or brush away specks.
If she ever threw salt over her left shoulder
it has not kept away bad luck.

This woman, my never asked-for aunt
has driven through Sunday
to sit on The Esplanade
and stare at salt-spray sea
till the soothe of it enters into her.

Sweet Peas

Breathing sweet peas
gives me my mother
and my old room:
polished linoleum
flowered curtains
that tatty pink
sheepskin on the floor.

I am the wooden doll
between her knees
as she twists and pins
unwilling hair
into snails
but in the morning,
blonde curls float through light.

Huddled in bed with fear,
I heard raised voices
thump the kitchen table
of their marriage:
his, rasping and strange
after our woman years
waiting out a jungle war,
hers, a sharper note.

In the same hard bed,
I was burning with fever
when she brought them,
a finery of moths
in violet, pink and blue,
restrained in a vase
nailed to my wall.

Wind-flowers

Down the pitted lane
the child kicked her stone,
kicking and muttering
*I hate the Japs, I hate
the Japs!* until
she stubbed her toe.
Her father was fighting
a jungle war
and almonds fell
about her head
in nineteen-forty-three.

The war is over now,
the family broken and gone.
A greying woman weeds her garden,
green and blowing with drifts
of Japanese wind-flowers.
She picks a few, pale-petalled
scraps of ricepaper,
and sets them afloat
in a glass bowl:
these fading letters
from her father.

Stalker

That shit, Insomnia,
who slept with my mother,
loved and left her for dead,
is shadowing me.
What a nerve.
Recalling her tense
and twitching step,
I brake my pace, feign calm.

The escape she made
is not for me
but then, you see,
I'm younger, lucky in love.
If that sly devil
comes stalking me
who knows, I may not
manage to shake him off.

It's taken me years
to hack away tangled
thorns and branches
covering her tracks.
Now the going is easy
even in the dark –
with my feet on the ground
her footprints are such a neat fit.

Legacies I

In July

These mornings of black frost
show me a younger self
in the bare unheated house.
It was hard July, when people die,
our telephone was screaming
as I ran down the passage
clutching a six-weeks baby
shivering from her bath
and wrapped up in a towel.

Folding her over my shoulder,
I tried to balance the phone
but froze to coldest ice
at unspeakable things
my sister barked
a thousand miles away:
Never mind the baby.
Mum's gone, an overdose.
Looks as if she meant to.
Outside, the fog came down.

Alone, abandoned,
I hugged the tiny child
my mother was coming to see,
stumbled and nearly fell
on our way back
down the corridor
to cold bath-water.

At this wry age I'm left
with a greed for babies.
I reach out hungry arms,
press them against my chest
and feel the body warmth,
scent rising from new skin.

Legacies II

My Father's Glasses

were square, brown-framed,
and not at all becoming,
the sort they wore in the seventies.
They came to me in a Gladstone bag,
its leather flaking off
like skin from a paperbark tree;
came with a red cigarette tin,
medals I wear on Anzac Day
and a wind-up watch, stopped.

When my sight began to let me down
driving in Roundabout City,
I tried the glasses on and found –
they matched the very lack
that was creeping up on me.
The glasses settled easily
were comforting, familiar,
if a little heavy
on a nose I had from him.
With them, I put my father on.
I didn't hope they'd bring
me any special wisdom,
after all, he let us down,
but looking with his eyes
I found myself clear-sighted,
able to see a way forward.

Last week I lost the glasses,
back came all the buried grief.
Nostalgia, too, for heatwave days
he used to take me fishing, nights
he played the Rheinberg upright;
for nicotine and aftershave,
his As You Were hair oil:
all the embarrassing ways of a dad
who drove a bomb with a canvas hood.

Again I'm the careless daughter
who's lost a precious book:
you always rush at things
like a bull at a gate, he said.
Without my driving glasses
once more I am bereft
of the faint recovered sense
of my best, unhappy, faithless father.

The Dwindling

The dead's beloved treasures dwindle.
First to go are the clothes they wore,
suits and ties and old-fashioned pants
are cleaned and packed for the Salvos' store.

After the war good cloth was scarce
so Grandpa's shirts became our blouses.
His furniture wasn't too easy to switch
as none of it fitted our post-war houses.

He left me a coin from Victoria's reign
to wear as a necklace, hung on a chain:
I lost it one day in the buffet car
while travelling north on the Sydney train.

One each from mother and two grandmothers
and best of all, are three old chairs.
They raise the tone of my modest home
with the *je ne sais quoi* of their antique airs.

There's the rocker, the tub, and the peacock blue,
their springs have sprung, their days are numbered;
horsehair in one makes my husband sneeze.
He says he no longer wants to be lumbered

but each old chair has a room in my head
and holds the shape of the woman who read there
so how can I hustle them off to the dump,
a squalid place with fetid air.

For down at the dump in Mugga Lane
tossed upside down with her skirt awry
is hardly the place for a stylish dame,
a prey to dealers who poke and pry.

My grandfather's clock has lost its chime –
it's tough when you linger past your time.

The Bone Tree

Night deepens and a tree grows
out of my cheek –
near the temple, in the bone.
Knotted roots strain under skin,
the branches seethe with birds
and a wind among the leaves
moans like a Greek widow
but the roots hold.

Twigs scratching the iron roof
begin a waking dream
of Grandma's house by the sea.
In darkened rooms
I touch her stiff-backed chairs
and sound the dinner gong,
hear its brassy boom.
Never speak at meals,
chew your food a hundred times.
Going down the cellar steps,
my candle's flame is fearful,
the damp breathes out of brick.
No wine in here, just rows of jam
in jars of amber, ruby, jet.

Upstairs again, the games of cards,
Snap and Switch and Fish.
But cards are the devil's playthings
and hide in a leather case
faking it as a book
with *A House of Cards*
embossed in gold on the spine.
Her cards held close to her chest,
Grandma's hands are soft as suede
and wrinkled walnut-brown.

Climb back down the bone tree
to summer-ripened fruit
and grapes weighing down the vines.
The moon's face is a grinning freak
and cockatoos fly calling
through the clouds, roost in my hair.

Private Museum

A collector and a connoisseur,
I am the sole curator
of my own domestic museum.
It's quite select, though small,
and growing all the time
but people may not handle goods.
I gloat on them alone.

Exhibit I

This woman's jewelled snuffbox
calls up a brown head bent
to sniff a frugal pinch
of tobacco crushed to powder
for solitary spasms
of secret sneezing bliss.

Exhibit II

The uncle's ancient secateurs,
patient on a peg, expect
the touch of callused hands,
quick to snip a half-dead rose
or one that merely nods;
adamant with privet hedge,
its eager thrusting shoots.

Exhibit III

The silver pendant earrings
of deep green chrysoprase
evoke my mother's nervous face:
the shadows on a ridge of bone,
her dark and deep-set eyes.
Too beautiful to fear betrayal,
she failed to see it coming.

Exhibit IV

Scraping off the wheelchair's rust,
my palms can feel the rubber grips
held to push a chair-bound friend.
I hear her shrieking laugh
sing rushing through the park –
all that unaccustomed wind
blowing back her hair.

Exhibit V

My father's ukulele
that he took away to war
is carved with names of soldier-mates.
The 'forties tunes that sing along
its yellow cat-gut strings
can roll back all his close-lipped years
before that crazy night
he raved of murderous Japs –
none of us were well equipped
to persuade him otherwise.

Exhibit VI

This sticky ice-cream stick
reeks of heat and summer light,
a splashing child in a pool
who is absolutely sure
it will never come to an end.

Perhaps it's by their deeds
that we may know men.
I'd rather read their relics,
and like to play a game:
display my precious hoard,
allow one second's glance,
then put them out of sight.
The trick is how to find a way
to keep the missing parts.

Night Shift

Waiting for light
I breathe in, and out.
There was a nightmare riding hard
its neck all flecked with sweat,
hoof-beat and heartbeat
thudding past my severed head
face upwards in a swamp.
I knew the sound of panic,
legs that would not move.

Thought brings no relief,
dawning fears are worse for being real.
Deadlines wait, and promises.
At last a peal of magpies
rinses morning air.
The spines of books are there
and other loyal friends – a trailing scarf,
the cushion on my waiting chair.

Outside, a gum's pale edge
stands firm behind the rose,
blurred in a vaguer space
of shrubs and shadow caves.
Somewhere a cistern sings
and now the blackbird can be seen
making her little darts and runs
across the wormy green.
Minute by minute
the grey gives way.
For light *does* come
and even, bursting
with hail-fellow, well met
grin, the sun!

The Dance

High on the hill this morning
hundreds of butterflies danced.
Flickering, sunlight-flooded
and lost in a mindless trance,
they blinked their golden wings
until each stem and branch
flowered with the fire.

As happens in those dreams
when one is caught unclothed
among a well-dressed crowd
I felt almost ashamed,
stumbling out of step
with the beat
of their flawless wings.

Trudging home again
to work and waking streets
I thought of a winter night –
saw chilblained hands,
a mouth full of pins
and the dark head of a woman
sewing silk for me.

The Birds

Our pallid winter days are marked
like commas on the sky's blank page
by passing strung-out flocks
of yellow-tailed black cockatoos.
Bold and clamorous they fly –
towards the sun at first light,
back through the western sky at dusk.

We wake to the sound of squeals,
contact calls as they beat a path
to the forest's rim on Mugga ridge.
Moving and murmuring,
they work through tree after tree,
stripping the bark for grubs in Red Gums,
gorging themselves on monkey nuts.

As the day draws in we hear them again,
shrill and sweet as children's play.
The sated birds go flapping home
to gullies in the hill behind the house.
The arc of their journeys defines our limits,
warns when it's time for the other world
or when to lower blinds, build up the fire
and crowd together in the roost.

Spoonbills, Wooli

Waiting for you
I watch the royal spoonbills
trawling up the river
like dancers in slim black tights.
A rainbow floods the birds with light,
transforming frothy skirts
to flamingo pink.
When the daylight drains away
they stand quite still and rapt,
each bird poised above itself
reflected like Narcissus
in the water's moonlit glass.

Out beyond the spit, the line of trees,
the surf is lying low.
The fishermen head for home,
tired and cold, gritty, wet.
Like heroes, they bring in the catch
and the tall tales:
'One of them ran with the line,'
you say, 'broke it under a rock.
A dozen were too small to keep –
but then this rainbow came
and washed the sea with pink
down to our line of rods along the shore.
It touched us all,
just before the light went.'

Timbarra

Dropping through dusk
is the deeper darkness
of the bird –
blue-black,
satin-sheened
bowerbird.
He watches from grevillea
with a lucid violet eye.
An eye to rival berries
by ferns and forest creeks,
that draws into its orbit
each trace of violet blue:
trinket or tinny thing,
feather from rosella,
frail shell of snail
or wing of butterfly
to deck the hall of straw
for his prancing dance
of love.
Magnetic eye,
drawing me out of time
beyond the ring of light.

The Weaver

I watched a red-browed finch
carry a load of fronds
above the swirling creek.

Again she flew and tore
the pale and tattered flags
of reeds along the bank.

The morning sun beat down
her work was slow and hard
but still she kept it up.

I walked across the bridge
to see what I could find
among the tangled scrub

though, lacking subtlety,
my work-boots blundered in,
no threat to privacy.

I never did detect
in twisting vine or tree
the warp and weft of a nest.

Uriarra

Under casuarinas
on a late-summer day
I watch a young echidna
pass along a pebbled rut.
She stops, deliberates,
hoists herself up rocks
and over twigs,
sometimes tips right
onto her back, to roll
from side to side, legs flailing,
before she rights herself
and carries on down to the river,
its water cool and brown.
Silently she sucks it in.

Going home, she meets my boot-soles:
leather-lidded eyes, dark nostrils,
but one touch, and knitting-needle quills
shoot up; she hunkers down.

My boots shift.
Echidna heads for the bank
unfazed by stumps or clumps of weeds,
by comical capsizing.
I stroke the pelt of belly fur,
her paws curl up in ecstasy.
More sideways flip
and waddle-toddle,
a stop to scratch, or snout about
for the odd, angry ant
and, just for the fun of it,
to kick up her back-to-front heels.

Platypus

The platypus at evening
flashes supple silver,
made fluid and mercurial
by tricks of light on fur
by trailing streams of bubbles
as she noses up for air.
The pool she dives is dark with weed
and dark her nervy muzzle
moving through the thickened shade
of a river bend at dusk.

The platypus in morning light
is a truer, denser brown
with sleek and thickly layered fur
and searching, dark brown eyes
in cavities of bone.
She flips on her back and dives,
comes up again to breathe –
and watch the stealthy watcher
who, half hidden by a rock,
is holding her own breath.

Meeeting the Psyllid

Craving light and winter sun,
I'm writing in the garden
when an insect flickers down
and meets my hurried scrawl:
the hot breath of the desert,
my black graffiti shout.
They dwarf the psyllid nymph,
lost in a waste of white
and wanting only sap to suck
from gum leaves overhead.

I bring a magnifying glass
to bear upon my visitor:
its curving saffron back,
bronzy wings of gauze
and two black crescents
drawn on a pin-top head.
I see it release a flow
of viscous white cream,
fabric to make a shelter
for the next growing stage.

I nudge the nymph towards the edge
but still it clings to words
those unambiguous signs,
hypnotic black on white.
A lizard slithers under bark,
I spin around to check…
and in that half a minute
my curious psyllid flies,
joins a hundred flecks of gold
climbing sunlit air.

Wistaria

Beyond my window's violet haze
the wistaria curtain shivers,
its flowers strings of glassy beads
lit by the morning sun.
Threading through the baubles
pass the bees, wearing sober brown
and lifted by the summer breeze
like creatures on a rising tide.
Crowds of bees will sip at sweetness,
float away and be replaced
with blithe unhurried ease
by others who will drink their fill
and dance in perfumed rooms
but always keep in mind
the hungry ones at home.
Behind the bees, the waiting hive
controlling all their moves.
Behind the flowers, the vine,
like a rope and knotted hard,
allowing just the briefest fling
before the winds of March
blast the fragile beads
and spill them on the grass.

Fossils, Wee Jasper

I kneel on the ground to peer
through the glass of a tiny lens
at the delicate trace of an eye
that glistened once, like mine.
This faint and concave print
of a primal eye that bulged
millions of years ago
is petrified and pitted,
the last unseeing trace
of a fish from before the time
when animals left the sea
to try the dryness of land.

Only the form remains,
with one nerve tunnel
brittle as teacher's chalk.
Yet this precise eye
can call up coral caves,
anemones and waving weed,
the dark shape of a shark
gliding swift and liquid.

Only ten such eyes exist
and six of them lie here
in rows of limestone humps
worn grey as the flanks
of enemies cruising an old sea bed.
I straighten and look up
to clouds, the sky, the cliff
with one circling hawk
scanning the land for prey.

Heat

Floorboards buckle and creak,
cicadas creep from rock-hard ground
to climb up trees for take-off.
The bark is flaking early.
Wings spread in a slit of shade,
magpies crouch and pant.
No tap drips, no grass runs green
to clods in garden beds.
Tired of grey-water rations,
geraniums wither and worms lie low,
there is no work for them to do.
The hopeful buds of roses
scorch before their time
while desolate hens
accept a dry dust-bath.

These mornings are not fresh;
along the widened cracks in walls
insects show their faces.
Men have ceased to whistle
and quarrels come to the boil.
In the thick uneasy silence
days dawdle to afternoons
and sleep that brings no rest.
Then women drag themselves
to the rack of stoves
while children pinch and fight,
biting the hand that feeds them.
No one wants to eat –
In this heat? they cry,
pushing away stale bread.

At kitchen sinks the sweat runs down
and pots and pans are slammed.
A sore breaks out along the lip
of a woman who would not dare
to waste the water for another shower.
Much more of this, she shouts –
I will, I swear I will.

This Rain

is pricking air
like needles stitching cloth,
it drips from the felted flanks of cows
and overflows bent pipes
that have lost the knack.
Pigeons' crests are battened down
and startled thornbills peer from twigs
behind their shower-curtains,
the wet we've all held out for.
Rain is a deeper sound on iron roofs,
on rubber boots and Driza-bones.
Old fogies rub their joints and look for liniment.

Borne on a wind, the rain has force:
umbrellas must cave in,
the stalks of flowers cringe
and rain drives under our guard,
stoical too long.
It drizzles into socks to find out ankles,
under collars to softest napes.
Clots of rain in the veins of clouds
smudge the line of hills, the valley floor.

Run-off sogs the drought's dry crust
and rain's leftovers lie about
quiet, drab, in puddle and dam,
resigned in the face of still more rain
sheeting down and pinning every thing
to a stillness of new green
and the liquid dark of trees come back to life.
We are undone, at last the tears come.

Eviction

We who love this house
and fan-shaped bit of land
are only tenants in our time,
content to share the place
with six old Blakely's Red Gums
set in a ring around us.
We're paid up with the rent
and suffer random visits from
the lordly sharp-eyed sun,
inspecting cupboards, stove,
a wild and tangled yard.

We play no raucous music,
tolerate the lechery
of other, feathered, tenants
on upper floors with views,
expect the same terms
as certain brush-tailed possums
that thump about upstairs.
Prowling the block like hungry beasts
are men in suits with plans.
We chuck tin cans and rocks
but they disperse to watch, re-group.

Rough as tanks, the dozers come
to churn up house, tree-bones
and tenant dust; they're making space
for glass-eyed cell-block towers
that rise to supervise the street.
No bird is left to sing the days
or swing along with the wind
like the old lot used to do
when the pearly shell of a moon
sat high in the crowns
of the trees who ran the place.

Prodigal Son

The frantic hullabaloo began with you
galloping up the steps to our waiting door.
Your talk was fast and flash, it rattled and flew
from roof to rafter, window back to floor.
Hardly a word escaped our open mouths,
hoping to make its cool, considered mark,
when ten of yours lit off on other paths
like bats come out to forage after dark.
You knew that we would always understand:
what drives you now is still that early death.
My kitchen thoughts were just what came to hand.
The racket warmed us from the winter's breath,
a winter long and bitter, true to form.
We brought you in and kept you from the storm.

The Trial

On days of leaden skies
when you are being driven
to meet your grown-up kids
you can be overcome
by a rising sense of dread,
a little like the fear
that seeps out of a criminal
on his way to court –
the pitiless jury and judge
are bound to find against
the hangdog prisoner in the dock.

They will condemn my sins,
my errors unwitting and witting,
those wrongly taken paths,
the unresisted rows;
will deplore a shameful record
and have no truck with parole.
It's too late for the lame excuse,
to attempt reform or argue a case
before these self-appointed
family court judges,
one's children.

For my Son

Do tell your son when he becomes a man:
as an embryo he made his queasy mother moan
but later his butterfly moving in the womb
filled her with bliss; your whole sleep-darkened room
glittered with a starry whirling light.
Say how close you lay that long sweet night
revelling in the novel shared delight
of waiting to see if he might flutter again, might
use this whispery speaking to you both
for months, until the drama of his birth
would end within the cradle of your arm.
You held him there: blinking, breathing, calm,
before you proudly gave him back to her,
you and she, the new-made father and mother.
And when the timid nibbles of nursing began
your tenderness spilled over and you ran
laughing and leaping out of the hospital ward
to telegraph the news around the world.
This story you must nourish and remember
for telling to our family's latest member.

The Scholar and the Wren

Walking to work in the library,
he climbs the grey slate steps.
A heavy bag is in his hand,
a thesis on his mind.
He fails to see the fairy wren
skittering through the rails
to hide in scented rosemary
where she will build her nest.
For while he sifts old papers
and studies arcane maps
to clarify the logic
of his academic feats
the wren will also pass a test
and raise a fine new brood.
From break of day
till the sun goes down
she flies to feed and guard
her clutch of blue-tailed facts.

Red Madonna

There's a woman asleep
sitting up, on the footpath,
in the photograph I took
that day in San Francisco.
The tall white church
across the road failed to see
her spread a straw mat
above the ventilation grid.

A thin red blanket
is folded and fastened
madonna-style
around her drooping head
and shoulders hunched
to lean against
nothing.
Her feet and stick legs
are wrapped in faded rags
like ancient mummies.
But somehow the grooves
in her closed brown face
and the downward line
of her lips protect
this practised sleeper
from the glassy stare and click
of strangers with cameras.

Sleeping woman,
you were so tired.
Have you slipped through
the iron ribs of that grid
while I've moved on
in another country,
your stolen image in my pocket.

Soup Kitchen

Down the road in Asphalt Gully
where derros meet the stoned,
a well scrubbed wooden table stands
beneath an old plane tree.

It's set up every Friday night
and laid with bread and cheese,
with stacks of polystyrene cups
set ready for the soup.

The kitchen's greasy makeshift floor
is swept by sharp-eyed birds
but Pola Jablonski is mother here,
her pantry's a kombi van.

At dusk, like shadow kangaroos,
the down-and-out appear,
come to graze with famished eyes
and wary, punctured arms.

Pola Jablonski at twenty-two
survived the worst of wars
when rats all fed on living flesh
and bred in empty skulls.

Tonight in headscarf and pinafore,
she rescues the lost and the sick,
saves the half-mad and rejected
with soup and thick buttered bread.

Cuisine Minceur

When eating out on trendy streets
you might catch sight of cockroach men,
their cigarette feelers waving.
In flapping sneakers, grey and limp,
they slink along with eyes cast down
from the bitter sight of munching mouths,
their hands shoved deep in fraying pockets
hooked on the bones of coat-rack hips.
It's a piece of luck if such a man
can snatch the sleep of restless days
on splintered benches in the parks
or under the arch of a concrete drain,
his bed made up with chips of glass.

But cockroach men come alive at night
in the city's darkened service lanes,
they watch the kitchens sweating grease
and do the rounds of garbage bins
left where chefs throw out their waste.
They know just when to glean among
the leavings of the glutted rich.
The species are hardly ever seen
by winers and diners at pavement cafés
who prize the hard-won privilege
to eat at tables neatly laid
above the cracks in dirty streets.
They are not obliged to live there.

Leaves

for Dorothy

As I walked up through Surry Hills
I met a woman, cobweb-grey,
hunched in the frame of her own doorway
and shivering from the winter's ills.

Wisps of hair blew round her ears,
from out there on the split footpath
I saw her empty chairs and hearth,
dingy from the wear of years.

It seemed as if she felt she should
keep an eye on passers-by
and so I stopped to find out why.
She watched, she said, to see who would

stop for a chat on her ninety-first,
although it had been yesterday,
'My cousin *said* he'd come today.
His health, like mine, is not the best.'

Her slipper poked a yellow leaf,
'It's these dead leaves that drive you mad.
When Council swept, it wasn't so bad.
Some poor soul will come to grief.

I'm never finished raking muck.'
Shifting on her crooked hips,
she sniffed and sucked in withered lips.
'You need a *truck* to pick 'em up.'

I left her then and made my way
to the pub on the hill with the neon sign
that promised a glass or two of wine
to drive all blighted leaves away.

The True Café

A blowfly in my coffee
in a café up The Cross
was not the sort of seasoning
you like to come across.

In those dark and narrow streets
there are drunks asleep in doorways
and I'm careful when I walk them
to refrain from looking sideways.

The rubbish in the gutters
is often on the nose
with dealers doing deals
where no cop ever goes.

The café I prefer has
four tables at their ease,
not too worn down by elbows
or kicked about the knees.

The regulars are few,
new customers are rare,
the thing that fills the place
is bluish smoky air.

The café's no more roomy
than a narrow alleyway
and it doesn't yield a living
though it's open night and day.

My friend who runs the joint
can barely pay the rent
her eyes are bleak and heavy,
her bony shoulders bent.

But her chessmen strut the board,
she lays the papers out
and the goulash that she serves
is spicy, rich and hot.

The Queue

The kids and claimants shuffle up the line
behind a bar that's painted on the floor.
A few have come to quibble at a fine
and others know they could be shown the door.
The down-at-heel in flaking thongs and jeans
are forced to join the frail and fearful old,
the genteel poor of lately straitened means
upset to find their income is on hold.

The harried desk staff, mindful of the clock,
still take the time to hide their private views.
They've learned the art of cushioning a shock
and dole out crumbs of disappointing news
while busy with a pen, a rubber stamp,
the tell-tale papers in a bulldog clamp.

The Skater

He cuts a fine figure at the conference,
skating cool and nonchalant
with one or two well placed cronies
over the literary ice, that glittering surface.
He's sure of drinks with the smarter people,
of never needing to eat alone,
and evades all hangers-on, or losers,
those humbler practitioners of the writing vice
with the unpleasant body odour of failure.

Beset by impressive commitments,
he arrives a little late, timing it nicely
for that exact point when the rink
is alive and moving with a good crowd
to observe his figures of eight.
But he always takes off early
before boredom freezes their faces
or stragglers catch at his sleeve
to remind him he skates on thin ice.

Yes, there can be the awkward season
when traitorous cracks appear
or the ice doesn't form at all;
when performers like him
may stumble and fall, are not called for.
Then he's astonished to find
that even his twists and turns,
for some strange reason,
have dropped right out of fashion.

Chica

I took her arm in the darkness
to guide her towards my gate.
Hey, I'm good in the dark, she said,
from the years behind the blindfold.
I was younger then,
my hair hung down to here.
I would like to give you names
but there was the blindfold.
They never let us see their faces.

Once, lying on other bodies
in the truck for the camp,
I saw through a crack
a trouser-leg, a gun…
Arms behind your head, they said.
Legs apart!
When they kicked me in the backside
I urinated and obeyed.
In the camp, Tejas Verdes,
my friends called me Chica,
meaning 'little one'.
We were Los Desaparecidos.

Wet sandbags were used –
my whole body turned
the colour of that wine
between us on your table.
On the day I signed
a knife was at my neck
and a gun was in my back.
I said I was happy
and did not mention the stink
of whisky and cologne on their skin
when they came…
or how I was stripped
and hung by my arms,
or the wires that were fixed
to my body's secret places.
A switch was pressed,
questions were asked.
Which I did not answer.
It is late. I am tired
from translating these things,
my language to yours.
After I left Tejas Verdes
my legs and arms, my head,
continued to tremble in spasms
like someone diseased.

The Burqa

2002

See the burqa woman
hampered by a shroud,
her character blanked out.
Woman, know your place –
a space more cramped
than any padded cell
for solitary confinement,
for raving nights of madness.
Even your cries are gagged
and the gaze of your eyes is fenced.

But your image has escaped
to speak of panic in the dark
and the many forms of malice.
It echoes the surreal –
those hooded, faceless,
figures by Magritte
that hint at nightmare
or the accused when dressed
and ready for the noose.

This black and white image
makes a lasting mark
upon my inner eye
but I walk quickly past
on the other side,
dazzled by the sunlight
my head in golden sand.

Kongarati Cave

(Second Valley, SA, 1934)

The men who unsealed your tomb
found a shrunken, smoke-dried corpse
bound in a foetal curve,
crusted salt had inscribed
the tissue-paper skin.
A woman swathed in seaweed,
your breasts were flattened
by the press of years
and wishbone elbows framed a gap
that might have been a nose.

Southern heat and air
began to mount their threat.
Before you crumbled into dust
a scholar measured you:
he made a charcoal sketch
and taking up his camera,
used the invading light
to save your fading look.
Printed on this yellowing page,
it takes me to your time.

Ramindjeri woman,
the rites have withered, too.
Layered sheep dung lines your cave
and no words ride your breath.
But Kongaratingga Creek
still sings a reedy song
pushing back the sand-choked bar
to dance into the sea.

Wangangu

In Warumungu country
the people walk barefoot,
their leather soles uncut
by thorn or flint or glass.
The brown and broken glass
winks from every shard,
a sharp unflinching glitter
on gutter, road, foot-path,
even the old bush track
that peters out at the edge:

as the light begins to thin
the drunken plastic bags,
these bloated white ghosts,
lean up against barbed wire
or dance with blonde grass
to a tune played at night
by jagged cans on stubbies.
They whisper to themselves
of things unspeakable:
kumunytyayi, kumunytyayi.

The Patriarch's House by the Sea

Imagining your voice where once you were,
I open doors to let in noise and light
and seem to feel your fiery spirit stir
as if you'd been arrested in mid-flight.
We loved to watch your animated face
defend a point of view with all your might,
your pounding fist that made our pulses race:
you liked to lead the family's mealtime rite.
A man who wanted argument and talk,
nothing held you back when you got going,
conducting with a glass or loaded fork.
Those times are gone. Now quietness is flowing
through empty rooms still waiting for your tread
and all the things that will remain unsaid.

Old Dubbo Gaol, 2004

In Dubbo Gaol
the stone is cold,
the window slits
are narrow.

Dark photos there
of eight they hanged
will crack your bones
to the marrow.

Their pallet beds
were knotted wood
with a blanket
but no pillow.

In Dubbo Gaol
the nights were long,
men's dreams all stank
of sorrow

for the pale ghost men
who faced the drop
with nothing at all
to follow.

Lament for London Bus No. 30, 2005

Turning a page of the local *Times*
I see a picture of the dead bus
under a blue tarpaulin shroud
and borne along on a semi for a bier.
The broken outline of its bulk
is sharp against the sky,
the people who were passengers
have vanished.

Without its usual rostered driver
the blameless double-decker bus
is making a last, post-mortem, trip.
Forensic teams will pick and scrape
at cavities and body parts:
they search for clues to the fatal ride,
for scraps of those who paid their fare
and died.

There is no grave for a bombed bus,
no priest reciting funeral rites
or friends with fulsome eulogies
who bring the flowers that fade.
And the working man who drove the bus,
hands on the wheel, steering a course?
They say he walked away unhurt
but haunted.

Voyeur

I love the allure of gates ajar,
of back-lit windows and promising doors
closed to strangers who drift on by:
the idle, the curious, the passing voyeur.

Rarely idle but very curious,
I always feel I have to know:
why the bearded man has turned
away from an interrupted woman,

one finger tensely poised
to mark her place on the open page;
why the little boy cries at the curtain,
with only a cat for comfort.

What makes the lovers, up in their flat,
shake such angry fists
at the dismal yellow shirt
hung out to dry on a length of rope?

And why does the girl in a red lace bra
frown and bite her nails,
hunched above her keyboard,
this hot and steamy Sydney night?

Their windows seem to invite my stare
but I call myself to heel and turn:
back to a houseful of hungry kids
and scum on the rim of the sink.

Where's the beckoning mystery
in any of that? And what's it worth,
content that simmers without surprise.
Must be more to it than meets the eyes.

Erhu Player, Sydney

He appears hardly real,
this patient Chinese fiddler
on the quay near his bucket
that's asking for my coins.
The man could be a figurine
moulded out of clay,
his meagre possessions
are stuffed in a bag.
Ferries hoot and wait to go,
tourists do their dough.

It's only when you hear
the high mosquito whine
of his wooden violin
that you know the man's alive
and coaxing ancient songs
from two taut strings.
There's a dislocated self
behind the glassed-in eyes
but his surface is undamaged –
what scars he bears are hidden.

I've read a scene like this before
in photographs by Hedda Hammer:
Peking, nineteen-forty-four.
Her black and white prints
echo here along the quay
in the erhu player with the antique air.
Other ferries wait to go,
more tourists do their dough,
he hopes to make a dollar
to pay his ferry fare.

The Ring Maker

for Berry

Through the celibate years
the ring maker stands at his bench.
He's chasing perfection
in silver, steel and wood
and builds new rings for flirts and lovers.
They bring the scent of other worlds
to break his mood with moonstone, jet
and slivers of petrified butterfly wing.

A lathe will spin the metal
against his meticulous tool:
the rings enhance and flatter
immaculate hands, mother-of-pearl nails,
but his are ingrained with dust
that flares above the bench.
He stoops to the task and squints,
a quiet, tense and focused arc.

When nerves beneath his collarbone
pinch and complain at night,
a surgeon with a knife and drill
cuts out a piece of bone.
The artist takes this core
and drives a hole through bone
pure and white as river stone
and fit for immortality,
fit to grace that finger
on his strong left hand.

The Bookbinder

The refurbished work imagined,
his rimless glasses glint above
the fractured spines of books:
he cuts out strips of kangaroo hide
to repair their crumbled calfskin
from days when books were rare,
the hand-sewn pages made to last.
Lacking a private studio
or even the aura of 'Artist at Work',
his quiet thoughts are nourished
by murmurs from his wife,
the slap and thump of her dough.

On a wooden kitchen table
he practises the craft.
Nothing flusters his knowing hand
or hurries his held breath
when lifting gold leaf wafers
for lettering the titles: one slip
and all must be done again –
the best letter in the right place.
At last a dead man's body of work,
now dressed in scarlet and black,
can speak to us without the risk
of falling apart unstitched.

On a morning of birds, the chance of sun,
he inspects the boards of *Humboldt's Tales*,
the diary of that curious German
who pushed the known world's edge
down to Peru in eighteen-thirty-one.
The bookbinder lifts tired eyes
beyond the window frame
and sees the raised arms of his wife
pegging shirts that whirl in the wind.
He flexes clever fingers
and marshals tools and glue,
ties on a work-stained apron to begin.

The Tide

Thassos, my Greek shoemaker
is a man who wears the pallor
of mushrooms grown in the dark.
All day and half of every night
he earns a sort of living
awash in the odour of glue,
standing and mending,
cobbling soles to uppers.
His hole-in-the-wall shop
is lined with cracked old shoes
all poking out their tongues.

An exile from Rhodos, island of roses,
he misses the warmth of sun on skin,
the waiting rows of coloured boats
and yellow fishing nets.
Lizard men who work the nets
will share a gritty coffee,
there's always plenty of time
to worry the beads through slackened fingers.

A dream of wealth and wider space
drew him to this cluttered cave.
A dream of islands pulls him back,
the suck and plash of waves.
It has become a tug of war.
On one shore are his parents,
living with their parents;
out here, the wife and children.
Neither side will give an inch.

The Model and her Model

i.m. Thea Proctor and George Lambert

for Anna

Within the frame, a man is seen to stare
and smile upon his 'fairest in the land'.
She twists a finger through her lustrous hair
and holds a kitten curled beneath one hand.
An open book lies ready on his knees,
perhaps some lines by Shelley, Byron, Keats
or Browning's *Sonnets from the Portuguese*
those ardent thoughts wrapped up in neat conceits.
Outside the room, a sky of midnight-blue
is hung with scattered stars and crescent moon.
He *seems* to court her, she to love him, too
but is there not a chaste and purer tune
that plays upon the minds of these old friends
who need each other for artistic ends?

Enid on the Sofa, 1957

i.m. Grace Cossington Smith

One afternoon of winter sun
dressed in her new red,
and the picture hat,
sparkling Enid Cambridge
bursts in to visit Grace.
She drapes herself along the sofa,
blissfully shuts her eyes
and basks in all that light
streaming through the window's lace.
Her body's dear familiar form
complements the cushions
and voluptuous curving chairs.

Seizing brush and paints
Grace works fast to get it down,
before her friend can stretch or yawn
like the sleepy cat she so resembles.
Colour within colour…
No clock ticks, no stranger comes
to invade the still, yellow room
and, like a post-card from a distant land,
the intimate mood is kept alive.
Today, a curious passing patron of art
may read its painted message:
'Dearest Enid,
from Mrs Van Gogh,
with love'.

Painted Lady

Awake in the thunder-broken night,
among a sediment of images
I see again a picture in a book:
the yellow nude reclines at ease
on rich embroidered silk.
Painted years ago in Paris
by a sad and stranded woman,
the work of art was wrapped
in swaddling clothes, laid in a crate
and sent home to Australia
for the brother of the artist.

His wife removed her troubled eyes
from the yellow-gold expanse of flesh,
this lolling Jezebel in oils.
The woman did not dare to dream
(though frightful dreams *did* come)
what such a baffling gift might mean
when given by a sister to her brother.
'Reclining Nude' was flung face down
on a wardrobe's upper shelf,
covered only by fluff and dust
in that arid, decent town.
The exiled artist died alone.
Her brother and his wife
lived carefully before they, too,
returned to dust, leaving behind
their hoards to be sorted and sold,
discovered by treasure-seekers.

And so I find the yellow nude
laid between the covers
of a cool and slippery book,
displayed for all the world to see
on thick white paper: smooth,
sweet-smelling with costliness.
Her body's lines are soft and round,
mocking silence and mere dust
to speak of languor and abandon
in sunny rooms, in Montparnasse.

The Collector

At eighty-nine in his scholar's book-lined cave
my friend avoids intrusive shafts of light
that sear and dazzle what remains of his sight,
the sight no surgeon's knife will ever save.
Though not the sort of man to whine or rave
he leads a sheltered life of endless night,
of sealed rooms, venetian blinds drawn tight.
What he can't have he's much too proud to crave.
I read aloud to him; my voice, his mind,
adrift among exotic tales. The vast
array of books has spurred a lifelong quest
for Chinese art – he always hoped to find
one perfect statue from the distant past
and holds the Buddha close against his chest.

Beguiled

Whenever I drive this hillside road
a certain bend invites me to fly
off and away from the edge,
to leave the shifting gravel rim
and turn my steering wheel
to air and freedom, Constable clouds.

I harbour an old repressed desire
from years of riding my bike:
the wind that gave wings to my turning feet
urged me to sail off the end
of a jetty across the sea
and soar with the wheeling gulls.

There is another place that waits,
the track to an old boat ramp.
Leading down to an inland lake,
it beckons me and wants my car
to skim the sedge like a water-ski
and glide with moorhen and duck.

Betrayal lies in wind and water,
the call of the sky is false.
Like sirens on a rock they sing
with sly, seductive arts –
which I resist, remembering
those roadside crosses and their flowers.

Harpy

See in your portrait
dark eyes like flowers
and strong writing hands,
shining hair, that searching look.
A year ago you were
the model sitter,
in your prime
on a summer morning.

Now you shuffle in, withered
no hair at all, mad staring eyes.
The past year has snatched
and flung you to the dogs
who devour you
leaving stick bones,
your remnant will
and strangely altered mind.

I'm reading the painting
of a woman I knew
who changed into a harpy
with the great wings,
the feet and tearing claws,
of a bird of prey.
Swooping,
you snap at the dogs.

Flesh and Bone

for Marian

I needed a sixth sense
that Spring before your last.
Your tulips had flowered and fallen,
the daffodils, jonquils, tazettas,
when suddenly you unbent,
gave me three bags full of bulbs
yielding, at last,
to my silent coveting.

In my chaotic garden,
unlike the terraced order
of your well-dug hillside beds,
a blaze of red and yellow,
their numbers slowly shrink:
from twenty last year
down to a sparse ten.
Although you taught me often
I can't tell jonquils from tazettas.

I've been searching for you
like someone lost in the bush,
half-blind with tears and sweat.
I suffered withdrawal
from a thirty-year addiction
to our friendship.
Life, they said, is a train ride:
you share the fun of the journey,
others get off; or you do
but the train travels on.
I told myself a darker tale.
A friend is like a coat
to ward off winter's cold.
There's a draught when it falls apart,
threadbare and full of holes.

I've cut a coat from other cloth –
it barely covers flesh and bone.

This late ragged spring,
an unexpected letter
from the far side of the world:
your spitfire daughter's wit
is sharp with irony,
the polished gift of story.
She even has your loyalty
and judgement sound as steel.

Two Good Men

Two men I knew have died this year,
shrunk to broomstick effigies and left.
Have I reached that awkward age
when the women on the bus are too many,
too scrawny and chicken-boned?
But the men, they ride free.
*Remember the hair on their wrists,
the deep sweet rumble of their voices.*
We named and counted their vices –
without them are poorer.

One was a slow-talking man,
pale eyes and a beard.
Lean and large-boned, he was good
with his hands – quiet hands.
A countryman from the start
he transferred a gentleness
with calves and lambs to the art
of printing, a life lived in suburbs.
I photographed his work boots once:
wrinkled, muddy, Van Gogh boots,
they talk about his honesty.
In the lonely gap between wives
he put the right word in the right place.

The other wore a cleft in his chin
and lover's lips. Scorn was his line
and recklessness.
Brought up tough in hard times,
he took the chip from his shoulder
and fashioned a blade to fell giants.
In the eye of the storm this giant-killer
rode the news screens of the nation
showing neither pity nor fear.
Nights he came roistering home
to wife and children; tender,
blue eyes full of the blarney,
the laughter and songs.

We women on the bus are too many
but the men, they ride free.

Flight

I am afraid, my friend,
that death is gaining on you.
All our clever strategies
have not concealed your footprints
from the demon tracker.
He casts a long shadow
and follows you fleeing
through grey corridors
and howling nights.
Smell his fetid breath,
he's gaining on you fast.
Your wit crackled and spat
but hasn't a hope
of outflanking him now.
At dawn the margin fades,
there is no light.
I hear the raven's moan,
its dying note awakes
the plaintive pardalote.
You falter and I wait,
fall back, reprieved,
to see you overtaken.

Seasons

Through summer's fickle omens
and the greying of the year
you sat it out with him
in spite of everything.

Although I know
it cannot be enough
I make you bread and soup
and wash four pears,
their sleek fat curves
like a Degas woman
bending over her bath.
I leave the brittle stalks
and peel sandpaper skin
until each pear is striped
in brown and white,
skin and under-skin,
ready to poach in syrup
of cinnamon, wine and cloves.
Upright in a shallow dish,
they lean together lazily
like the sculpted pears
set in the gallery's garden.

Death has come to the dying year.
The pears huddle together, whisper
of running juice and ripened flesh,
but clouds hang over the lake
and a wind knocks into shape
the menacing gun-metal waves.

Under the Jacaranda Tree

The unseen crescent child
burrows in your cradled belly,
turns away from hinted space
and into musky dusk.
Swirling grey enfolds the baby,
tones of light and shade.
Like a tight-curled tendril
she clings to what is known,
its back and forth swing
and smooth gliding slide:
the starting-place,
a slippery slope.

New Baby

for Glenn

She seemed to be content,
by herself on the other side,
but now she has come through
and listens to their voices murmur
sees the faces loom.
From up above and like the rain,
hair is falling softly on her head.
She tastes the sweet and sticky stuff
hearing as she breathes and sucks,
a beating she knows well
from when she was alone
without the risk of room to move.
Her father's finger on her palm is warm
and she holds fast, decides she wants to stay.

Inheritance

On the day that you were born
I held you in my arms
and saw my father's face
faintly stamped on yours.
I worried about the nose.
The first impression changed,
replaced by looks and ways
peculiar to yourself.
All that's left to show
you are his heir
is the half-moon curve
of your eyes in a smile
and a prettier print
of the rounded nose.
About him I have mixed feelings
but you are flesh of my flesh
and mother of this laughing child
with her own rounded,
curious, upturned nose,
dark eyes that dance with light.

Grandmother

This is the grandmother I shall be:
I'll sing you a crooning lullaby tune
and offer you fruit on a silver spoon.
If I hear you cry I'll find the moon
and raise you high so you can see.

When you become a noisy girl
we'll kick up our heels and both run wild.
I'm not the sort to be meek and mild
when babysitting my dearest child.
A groovy gran is best for a girl,

a groovy gran in purple socks,
a slave to fashion I'll never be.
I'll cook your favourite food for tea
and tell you stories on my knee.
I'll be the gran that nothing shocks.

Slowly we'll change. It'll be your turn
to teach me all the modern tricks
and lend a hand with things I can't fix.
By then I shall need two walking sticks
but you won't be too old to learn.

Even though it won't be the same
you can play me a sweet romantic tune,
feed me mush with a patient spoon
or drive me out to look at the moon
when I'm feeling lumpy, looney and lame.

What Women Want

There's something about the act of feeding –
two needs that meet with a soundless click.
It's why the centuries of art that show us
giving breast to babies never palled,
why crazy ladies foster cats who must be fed.
We love to scatter grain to chooks and feel compelled
to offer crusts to ducks who swim in questing circles.
It is why the kettle is always on the boil.
The anorexic vegetarians understand,
refusing is one of their weapons.
Just a muttered 'none for me, thanks,'
and the would-be good fall back defeated,
consoled by the scarlet throats of magpies
begging for gobfuls of worms,
by the clink of coins in a busker's hat,
or even the sight of a mother, kneeling,
to hand her child an ice cream.

Rushcutters Walk

Baby, did you *know*
there's a mother on your back,
a tall, strong backpack?
She goes everywhere you go.

You love these signs of bay-side life:
dogs that run to sniff the grass,
joggers swerving as they pass,
the buzz and roar of traffic strife.

Warmed and dazzled by the light,
you watch the yachts across the water.
Your mother is my sturdy daughter
strapped behind you, snug and tight.

With a mother on your back, you're freed
to wave at all the faces
and take in these new places –
she has just the elevation you need.

Under the Magnolia Tree

The spirit of the growing child
fills the house beside the tree,
darkest green at summer's end
and hung with lamps of crimson fruit.
The tree belongs to the house on stilts,
its wide verandas and slatted light
that stripes the back of the crawling child
exploring a world beyond our arms.
She tastes a hinge, an emerald ring,
swaying silk on a tasselled shawl
and stalks the painted toes of passing feet.

Below in the secret forest of grass
she finds the fallen cones
of dried magnolia fruit,
bristling with thorns all set to prick
and packed with seeds as bright as blood.

The child looks up at the sound of the bird
who sings the green magnolia tree:
'Ko-el, ko-el, come mate with me
come *in,* come *in.* Ko-el, ko-el.'
His song is descant to the wind
that blows up from the bay,
blows through the green magnolia tree
on singing bird, stalking child
and seeds as berry-bright as blood.

After Vermeer

It's just about a fortnight since
seized by a mood of burning lust
to tidy up, to wash and rinse
my kitchen floor of smears and dust,

I fell on my unpractised knees
and scrubbed away the sordid signs
of cooking, age, and splattered grease.
I took great care with all the lines

that separated black from white
working till each chequered square
shone with artistry and light,
a stainless clarity too rare.

Soon, upright on triumphant feet,
the smiling child comes walking there.
She greets the tiles as a special treat,
her friends from days of crawling where

she wished to go, and hugs my floor,
lays on it a sleep-flushed cheek
as if life could offer nothing more –
and sighs, so moved she cannot speak.

www.ingramcontent.com/pod-product-compliance
Lightning Source LLC
Chambersburg PA
CBHW070931080526
44589CB00013B/1475